KNUTE SKINNER

What Trudy Knows
and Other Poems

SALMON POETRY

The characters in these poems are all fictitious

Published in 1994 by
Salmon Publishing Ltd,
Upper Fairhill, Galway
A division of Poolbeg Enterprises Ltd

The Publishers gratefully acknowledge the assistance of The Arts Council

The moral right of the author has been asserted.

A catalogue record for this book is available from the British Library.

ISBN 1 897648 22 7

Cover illustration by Sue Smickler
Cover design by Poolbeg Group Services Ltd
Set by Poolbeg Group Services Ltd in Palatino 10.5/14
Printed by Colour Books, Baldoyle Industrial Estate, Dublin 13

To Edna Faye

Acknowledgements

Some of these poems have appeared in the following periodicals: *Agenda, American Literary Review, Djinni, The Burren Meitheal, Footprints on the Limestone, Fortnight, Imago, Iron, Jeopardy, The New York Quarterly, The Next Parish Over*: *A Collection of Irish-American Writing* (New Rivers Press), *Of Ordinary Lives and Stones*: *Departures 5, Orbis, Poetry Motel, Seattle Review, Southern Review, Stet, This Is Where We Came In,* and *University of Windsor Review.*

Contents

What Trudy Knows

I find myself mourning
but not for anyone we have buried
and not for the old neighbourhood
or my lost youth
or any of that crap.
To make no bones about it
I am mourning myself.

Trudy doesn't get it at all.
When she lays her head on my chest
and her yellow hair lies loose
all over my stomach,
I still turn over her way
and I do my homework.
But she knows it isn't the same—
even as I enter her body she knows
I am going through the motions.

It's easier at work.
I can laugh at my buddies' jokes
and tell a few of my own
when we break for coffee
and no one's the wiser.
The boss as always can see
I clock in on time.

But I know and Trudy knows
that the man who took up space in this world
under my name
has slipped out the door without so much
as a by-your-leave.

How she sticks it I don't know
but we have our meals as usual
and we visit her folks as usual
and we go to the movies or go bowling
and we fight about money we don't have
for the new baby
and it's only the odd time that I catch her
looking at me when she doesn't see I see her
and I know she knows.

A Well Lit Room

The rain rattles against the window so hard
that I look up from my book.
"They're trying to get inside," I think.
"It's like the night that they came
for my next-door neighbour."

But the room is lit by a bulb overhead
as well as my gooseneck lamp.
A red fire glows on the hearth.

A young woman in my book is falling in love
with the city attorney who seems to think
she has spread false rumours about his client.
Well, I still have over a hundred pages to go,
and within that compass will come
a happy ending.

The lights fade out but then gradually return;
my hands relax their tightened grip on the book.
The rain beats harder against the window,
but the lights, now brighter than they were,
reflect from the large mirror over the mantel.
I will turn the pages slowly and pass this night.
They can stay out there in the dark
where they belong.

A Walk in the Rain

We walked out of the bar without a word.
What needed to be said?
Behind us, the lively sound
of fiddle and flute
and a blur of voices
not unlike
responses in church.
Before us, a three-quarter moon,
for the moment released from the hold
of drifting clouds.

It was a warm night in September,
just days till holiday's end.
For a time the rain had turned soft,
and a breeze passed over the wet
cobblestone street.
The lamppost ahead cast a path
of light down the pavement.

At the corner we paused a moment
beneath the lamppost,
and we turned toward one another.
Her brown eyes shone bright,
and the smile on her parted lips
seemed an invitation.
"This is almost too easy," I thought,
not bothering to ask myself
what she may have been thinking.

4

Then I kissed her the second time—
the first time had been in the bar—
and she answered my kiss in turn,
there beneath the lamppost.
A passer-by stepped around us,
out onto the cobblestones,
with a cheery good night.
Then I slid a hand under her jumper,
and for the first time I smoothed
my hand on her back.

"Let's keep on walking," she said.
So we passed that night together,
as you might have supposed,
and then three of the four remaining
nights of my stay.
That was two brief years ago now,
and on rainy nights
I can close my eyes and I hear,
as from a doorway behind me,
the sound of fiddle and flute
and a blur of voices.
Then sometimes I ask her out
for a walk in the rain.

A Teapot with Character

"Now that is a teapot with character," I said,
as she picked it up from the table.

"This old broken spout, you mean? Our germ catcher?
I wouldn't call that character," she replied.
She dumped out the tea bags in the bin
and placed the teapot on the counter.
"Now in town there's a teapot and cups and saucers,
a whole tea set, mind you,
that has desperate character.
It's green and pink and has men on horses
crossing a narrow bridge into a village
that looks like a scene from the telly.

"Oh it's lovely," she said, and she paused by the sink
with a dreamy smile on her lips.
Her red curls were tied back from her round red face
by a blue ribbon with silver crescents,
and as she described the tea set,
she looked like a girl.

"I can buy it for half nothing," she continued,
"when I've saved enough tokens."
She lifted the plain brown teapot again
and ran her finger over the broken spout.
"Mind you, it could take me a year," she said,
"with only the two of us home,"
and she put it back down.

I stubbed my cigarette out and rose from the table.
"I'd best be running along," I told her,
"before they send out the dogs to find me.
Thanks for the tea."

"Oh for nothing," she said, wiping her hands on her apron.
"It was only some old brown bread.
Next time you call I'll give you a proper tea."

"It was lovely," I told her. "Your brown bread is gorgeous."
I put my jacket on and crossed to the door.
"Tell Josie I was asking after her," I said,
"and thanks again for the tea."

"For nothing," she said. "For nothing.
Next time you call I'll give you a proper tea."

I stood in the doorway a moment, half undecided.
"I use the same brand of tea," I said.
"I could give you my tokens."

7

The Streets toward the River

I made my way as quickly as I could
down the narrow streets toward the river.
I tried to keep close to the dark buildings,
but even there the wind found me out.
The April rainers were done with their downpour,
but the cold night air was still wet
with their gusty spatters.

Somewhere, if Al Jolson had it right,
gardens of grateful seeds were preparing for May.
I had my own May to think about
and my own reasons for being grateful.

The streets were empty of life,
but the old warehouses, scary at any time,
were grim observers of the lightless sky.
Nothing, however, could alter the mood of my youth
or the long-yearned-for promise of love.

And sure enough, I was soon at my goal,
the sheltered stop for the disused ferry.
May stood there waiting—cold, eager, and wet.

We'd be too careful these days to meet at night
in that part of the city in any weather.
But that night all we could think of was kissing,
and breathing hot breath on each other's neck,
and warming our hands under the thick wool
of each other's sweater.

Stale Biscuits

I quickened my steps until I saw the cottage
and then paused at the crab tree
beside the gate.
Though it was a short three miles from the cross
where the bus had dropped me,
my breath was coming in bursts. My mouth was dry.

In the garden a few ambitious chickens
scratched about in the weeds and tall grass.
The door to the shed hung loose
from a broken hinge.
Had it been only two years
since my last visit?

There was no sign of my grandfather's dog,
and I stood unannounced in the doorway.
The old man looked up from his chair,
his troubled eyes adjusting to the figure
framed in the light.
"Ah, Derek … yes, Derek," he said. "Come in, come in."

My mother's letter was there before me,
propped against the clock on the dark mantel,
a conspicuous white.
It looked larger each time I glanced up from the table
where Grandfather poured tea with a resolute hand
and told me to eat another of his stale biscuits.

Smiling

I smiled, but the smile was as rotten
as the taste in my mouth.
Roger would have smiled the same
if he too had been privileged to see
their skulky expressions.
If the dead could smile.

Here's what they looked like.
(This much I do remember.)
Jackson was wearing the paisley shirt
that Bea bought for Roger that day
he quit his job at the feed store.
Bea was in the yellow-green dress
that I helped her pick out
from the sales rack at Spender's.
Though it was a warm May morning,
they were both carrying their jackets.

Through the screen door I could make out
Jackson's car standing ready
at the bottom of the walk.
I didn't have to look into their room
to know they were leaving.

They had their last sight of me then.
I suppose I looked like death warmed over
in my terry cloth robe
and my hair a mess.
I hadn't washed sleep from my eyes,
or blown my nose,
or even had time
to empty my bladder.

10

But they thought of everything, they did.
They'd taken the shopping list and all,
and they said they were coming back
with a big surprise.
Skulky as they tried to be,
they probably knew I'd wake up.

I can't remember much else,
though I keep thinking that if I could
it might help somehow.
I stepped through the mess on the floor
and stood by the window.
I just stood there smiling,
and I waved from the window as they shot off
in the old Ford.

After the accident, the police
made me go with them
to view the bodies.
Later in the day,
I found a small framed picture of Roger.
Under the kitchen sink.
In a sack of trash.

Sleep

Awakening from a sensuous sleep,
I found it unnecessary at first
to fashion myself.
No subject proved forceful enough
to make me regain the glossy
territory of thought.

So I slipped instead
into a sea of endless stretching.
My limbs luxuriated as my mind
played with one photomontage
after another.

It was too good to last, of course,
and it ended at once with the housekeeper's
call to breakfast.
My room was still cold,
and it took me perhaps a minute
to locate my slippers.

Downstairs, I found all
the same as before.
My wife had been given no sudden, magnificent cure
for diabetes.
My daughter's account of her soul remained
a barefaced lie.
And my sister's countenance of hard rubber
repeated somehow the miracle
of mastication.

Sleep for awhile may knit up,
as the poet has it,
the ravelled sleeve of care;
but sooner or later my obtrusive life
will drag its ass to the surface once again
and hang out its shingle.

Sitting Up in Bed

I sat up in bed and reached for the light switch,
but nothing had changed.
My bag lay on the stand in the corner
just where the porter had placed it.
None of the contents of my pockets—
an amalgam of matches, money and cigarettes—
had moved from the spot where I'd lined them up
on the edge of the dresser.

I sat on the edge of the bed,
my eyes on the locked door.
Then I switched off the light and lay down.
"Gosh," was my thought. "Gosh."

After awhile I sat up in bed again
and reached for the light switch.
Nothing had changed.
My bag lay on the stand in the corner
where the porter had placed it.
None of the contents of my pockets, *etcetera, etcetera* ....
You know how it goes.

I sat on the edge of the bed,
my eyes on the locked window.
A gross shape was moving
on the edge of the sash.
It was just discernible in the nearly authentic dark,
and I saw it was only a shrub.

"Gosh" is a silly word,
it's a child's word,
but I said it this time out loud.
Then I switched off the light and lay down.

Once more I could hear faint strains
emerge from the night
as from the constricted throat
of a madrigalist.

I sat up in bed,
and I reached for the light switch,
and I sat on the edge of the bed.

Sick

I awoke at five, felt
very sick, and was sick.
The sun had burst through leaves
of the old hickory,
stippling the swimming pool.
Shards of a glass sparkled
along the pavement's edge.
One towel swam in water
and one snugged against me,
sprawling beside a chair.

My car keys were missing,
and Jayne-Anne was missing.

I ran a hand through warm
water in a puddle,
feeling some comfort there.
The sky looked a muddled
tint of robin's-egg blue.
Nothing ever did go
the way I had it planned.
The sun would be hot soon,
and I would be sicker.

Salvation

Enough is enough,
and I'd had enough of their kind already.
I hated their clean, dark, cheap, conservative suits.
I hated their ties, their white shirts.
"I don't need your help," I shouted;
"I'm as saved as you are."

All that, of course, was a lie,
but it felt so good to say it
that I said it again on my way to the kitchen.

Then I said it again over two cups of coffee.
And again and again through a hot bath.
And lying down on the bed with a new novel,
the curtains closed against an obtrusive sun,
I said it once more.

But the pages of the book have blurred.
Oh true apostles, somewhere, come ring my bell.
Open my door.

The Roman Centurion

As a Roman centurion I didn't much like
(so Juanita has told me)
the duties I had to perform.

But always I did them.

And that's what I try to tell Robin
whenever he raises a fuss
about his assignments.
Like tonight, when he can't stand the thought
of sex with Zimansky.
"He's fat and he's gross," Robin tells me,
pouting as he fingers his curls,
"and he belches and farts."

Our hotel room looks out on the courts
where all afternoon Robin has been so splendid,
racing his lithe blond body forward and back,
bestowing defeat with uncanny grace
set after set.

Now he looks at his image and chooses a crystal
    pendant
to go with his perfect tan.
"And Owen tells me," he says, "that Zimansky
takes forever to come."
I stand up behind him and fasten his clasp.

Robin takes a deep breath and catches my eye.
"Do I have to?" he says to me,
his voice growing small.

"No, it's all right," I tell him,
stroking the curls at the back of his neck.
"I'll do Zimansky."

A Promise

"I can't promise you poetry,"
the man's voice said,
"but I can promise a dandy spring day."

"What's this all about?" I answered.
"To whom am I speaking?"

"To someone who wants a picnic down by the lake.
You bring the potato salad and the chicken.
I'll bring the wine."

"How will I know you," I said,
falling into the mood,
"if you won't let me know who you are?
You do sound familiar."

"Oh, you can bet I'm familiar.
Familiar enough with the lake at any rate.
May I get familiar with you?"

"As familiar as the phone allows," I replied,
"and if you'll excuse me now, I have work to get back to.
I'm rolling up a dead body in an old carpet."

"Oh, of course," came the voice, "and by the way,
in case no one's told you this morning,
you're looking just lovely."

A Pretty Picture

When the band starts up,
we rise to join the crush of bodies
on the small floor
where we jiggle and bounce to the music.
When they finish the set, her long brown bangs
are plastered against the shine
on her red face.
I take her hand to lead her back to the table,
and she squeezes her stubby moist fingers
into my palm.

At the table I fill two glasses of gassy beer,
then cool my hands on the pitcher.
She smiles and presses a glass
up against her cheek.
"That's a pretty picture," I say
and look from her cheek to her large brown eyes
and her small red mouth.
I still can't think who it is
she reminds me of,
but she pats my hand and she smiles again.
"Save my place for me, Sweetie," she says,
"while I visit the sandbox."

As she moves through the crowded tables,
I stare at the back of her compact body
and admire her evasive tactics as hands reach out.
They grab at her yellow blouse
and the rear of her tight white jeans
till she passes from view.

I take out my wallet and count the bills.
I fan my face with a plastic bar menu.
A passing drunk spills beer on my shoulder
and then spills some more on my foot,
saying he's sorry.
And then she is back again, taking both my hands
and urging me up on my feet.
"They're playing our song, Sweetie," she says,
and I laugh out loud—
delighted to learn that she also has
a sense of humour.

A Pressed Blue Suit

I stood behind a pressed blue suit
and bright black shoes.
At the lectern a minister of state
was making a point.
Curls of silver-grey hair
met a blue-striped collar.

The minister made his point, and the crowded hall
erupted in laughter and applause.
The arms of the pressed blue suit
moved closer to its sides,
and its shoulders shook with the rhythm
of striking palms.
Silver-grey curls bounced on and off
the back of the blue suit coat.

The minister lifted his eyes from his paper
and bestowed an appreciative smile.

A Place at the Table

She took a place opposite me at the table
and prepared to eat.
She buttered her potatoes and peppered her green
        beans;
she covered her spareribs with salt.
Then she stretched her fleshy arm over the table
for the pitcher of water
when it would have been just as easy
to ask me to pass it.

Did she really assume that I would speak first?

Across the room the president's special assistant
was adjusting the mikes
while the group at the head table
responded with easy laughter.
When we noticed each other looking that way,
we returned to our plates.

She was well ahead of me there.
Except for the bones, she'd eaten all of her ribs,
even the fat,
and she mopped up the last of her mashed potato
with a slice of white bread.
Her new ring looked smug on her pudgy finger.

At last the servers came, passing out coffee,
and one of them whisked away my half-eaten meal.
Some of the other half
(it was some of the mashed potato—for the record)

had fallen on my shirt and tie.
But she lost interest as soon as the judges announced
the several awards.
She didn't, thank goodness, receive one.
Neither of us did.

She was wearing—for the record—a blue dress,
and something in the fabric glittered.
It fit her well and it showed off to advantage
her generous bust.
A chain of gold enhanced the warm flow
of her tanned skin,
and in spite of myself, she made me ache.

And, in spite of myself, she finally heard me tell her
it was good to see her again.
She nodded her head in the briefest of recognitions.
"Yes, but it's just like old times," she remarked:
"you were never much fun at dinner."

New Roses

The first few days
I slept as much as I could,
which wasn't easy with Matt at home
tiptoeing in and out of the bedroom,
bringing new roses and checking to see
if I'd taken my pills.
And, Lord, the look on his face
as he fussed with my covers
and asked if I was all right.

But he never did ask me the question
he wanted to ask,
and as often as he tiptoed in,
he never stayed long.

I slept as much as I could,
and sometimes in sleep I walked freely
through spacious, tapestried rooms,
or I ran with ease over fields
bright yellow with celandines.
And sometimes I lay stock-still
on a dark, cold floor—it could be in a cave—
and whimpered as numerous wings
brushed over my body.

Then Matt would appear again,
replacing the day-old roses,
rearranging the pillows,
and asking me once again
if I was all right.

My Mother's Number

I went into the bedroom and called my mother's number.
There was no answer of course.
I listened while the phone rang ten times,
as I once heard is correct,
but still there was no answer.

As always Ernie's bedroom made me nervous,
with its paintings of sailboats, its sculptured dogs,
and the Varga Girl prints Ernie found at an auction,
still in their bright pink frames.
On the desk stood a black and white photo of Ernie
with the boys of his lodge.

In the kitchen my hero was mixing up cocktails.
I could hear his blender and the shaking of ice.
In a minute Ernie would holler out to me
in a voice too loud for his small apartment.
"Hey, Sugar," he'd say, "whatcha doing?
There's a drink here with your name on the cherry,
and it's yours for a smile."

I checked my face in the mirror over his dresser
and ran my hands down the sides of my skirt.
Then I picked up the phone and called my mother's number.
I could hear Ernie placing our glasses on a tray,
and I tried to imagine the telephones all ringing
in room after room of the vacant house.

Mushrooms Berkeley

Somewhere an accountant was driving home
from fiddling the books in a closed-up shop,
but we were about to have a late-night supper
after a not-so-good movie.

Our conversation, such as it was, passed
on and off over the checkered cloth
on the small table by the window
in his almost-as-small kitchen.

We had talked the movie to death, and now
I looked out his window at the scene below.
A couple was standing, their car door open, and kissing,
unaware perhaps that somewhere a hospital nurse
was dealing in drugs.

I can't help it, I think this way,
but the wine he had poured was tasty enough,
and I was enjoying the smell of food
that came from his small stove.

"We can eat now," he said, as if reading my mind,
and pushed back his chair to rise from the table—
just as, no doubt about it, somewhere
a rapist stood up from his bleeding victim.
This isn't an easy way to go through life.

"It's probably evil but not dark," he said,
lifting a lid from a saucepan.

"What are you talking about?" I asked,
startled and probing the bland features
of his wide-open face.

"Mushrooms Berkeley," he said,
dishing up our plates.
"It should look dark and evil, according to the cookbook,
but mine never comes out dark."

More Tea

"Sunday papers and the afternoon match
weigh heavy on my heart," I said.
"Yes, I suppose so," he replied,
turning a page of the paper without looking up.
I gathered the breakfast plates
and headed for the kitchen.
"More tea?" I called from the doorway.
"Yes, please," he answered.

I put the water on the boil and looked out a window.
Rain was falling on the greenhouse glass
and the corrugated roof of the shed,
but the radio had promised a change.
The afternoon, it said, would come bright and sunny,
and I pictured the green filling up with children
and couples with closed umbrellas.

"Did you hear what I said?" I asked him
as I brought in the tea.
"You asked if I wanted more tea," he said,
stretching and letting the paper
slide to the floor.

"No, listen," I said. "I said
that the Sunday papers and the afternoon match
weigh heavy on my heart."
Just then a powerful burst of rain hit the windows,
my only round of applause.

In the silence that followed, the sun came out,
and he carefully spooned his sugar before looking up.
"But we always read the papers," he said mildly,
"and you know that we always make a point
of watching the match."

I spooned some sugar in my own tea.
"I know," I answered.

A Lousy Mess

I rubbed a hand over my bristled face
till I came to the spot on my cheek
where Randy had hit me.
I laughed remembering how
I had hit him back.
Maybe Randy wasn't feeling
so good himself.

I walked across the kitchen,
stepping over peanut shells
and kicking aside butts
from an overturned ash tray.
I pulled back the curtains.

The rain was falling in buckets, thank God;
there'd be no practice.
I puked in the sink.

When I finished puking, I ran cold water
and splashed it over my face
and rinsed out my mouth.
Maybe that made me feel
that I'd almost live.

If I did live, I'd have a lousy job
cleaning up the room.
With the broken glasses, the spilled beer,
the scattered popcorn and the bloody towels,
maybe it was one lousy mess.

I saw by the clock I had almost two hours
till I had to meet Katie's bus.
I opened the door and pissed out in the rain,
and then I went back to bed.

A Long Time

"It's been a long time," Jeremy said,
taking Stephanie's hand and bending
to kiss her cheek.
A bit stiffly, I thought.

She broke away and looked past Jeremy
to where the rest of us mortals stood
waiting our turns.
Recognition chased doubt across
her glamourous features.

She noticed my presence at once, I was certain,
though she turned her attention quickly
to her Aunt Carolyn.
She received the proffered hand with a smile
and her old thrilling laugh.
"How are you, Auntie?" she asked, embracing.

"Here, let Jeremy take your coat," said Carolyn,
"and come inside where we can see you.
You're still the same Stephanie, I'll warrant,
though the years have taken their toll
inside these walls."

Yes, it's been a long time, I thought,
as Stephanie handed her coat to Jeremy
and then skipped over to my brother Will.
And why, I thought, were we all standing attendance
like a pack of old fools?

The biggest fool of all, I was wearing a tie
that I had hoped Stephanie would remember.
Turning to Martha, I found her hand and held it,
as much for my own reassurance as for hers.

The Long Path

I parked our Ford coupe on the dirt road
and, careful to raise as little dust as I could,
led Carla up the long path.
Chickens, scrabbling in the yellow grass,
scattered to the side.

Carla had on her plucky look,
which suited her better than her makeup.
No doubt she needed them both.
I wore what I foolishly hoped
was an easy smile.

That was forty-some years ago.
The sun was hot as a furnace, as my soul knew
but my neck and shoulders had forgot.
The withered and paint-cracked shutters
hung loose on their hinges,
positioned as they had been disposed
by the last, interrupting wind.
Two dark figures sat slumped on the stoop,
the two begetters of all I have begot,
expressionless eyes expressing
rancour and fear.

I visit the graves sometimes, always alone
except for my driver.
We left that day with a blessing of sorts,
a half dozen eggs and a rueful prayer
for our dubious junction.

Long Hair and Serious Eyes

"Is the old man still alive?" I asked,
as I poked some more small holes
in the newly dug earth.
The furrow hadn't yet dried, and mud
stuck to my boots as I moved along.
The day, however, was fine, and we had
the promise of fine days to follow.

She didn't answer at first, as was her way,
and I stopped to watch as she carefully placed
each hopeful pea seed in a new hole
and then covered it over with her gloved fingers.
Her body was lost in her loose, dark clothes,
and a floppy hat that shaded her eyes
hid most of her face.
Her long curls, however, passed over her shoulders,
at times almost touching the ground.
I saw and was sharply reminded
of the day before when I buried
my troubled face in that same long hair,
before taking comfort in her flesh.

Mud was on her boots as well,
and also on her knees,
but the sun was bright and the air almost warm.
She straightened her back, and as she lifted her head,
I could see again the warm colour
in her serious eyes.
"I don't know," she told me, shading those eyes
with a gloved hand.
"He was the last time I saw him."

Keeping Warm

"Doesn't life get shorter by the minute?"
I turned to locate the speaker,
impressed by the audacity
of the cliché.

What I saw was a spare old man
speaking into his pint
and letting our end of the bar listen in
as he talked to himself.

Outside a promising season had clouded over.
Inside a man in an unlikely Mexican vest
was urging on me a whiskey I only half wanted.
It was his birthday, he said.

Along the bar there were men keeping warm
in the company of laughter and drink.
Then a new one came in from the rain.

"Whatcha drinking, craychur?" the pretty
young bargirl asked him—
still dressed in her school uniform—

and "Mercy Bee Coo," she said to the birthday man
as he paid for my whiskey.

The spare old man looked up at her from his pint.
"Doesn't life get shorter by the minute?"
he asked her.

Keeping One's Wits

Denis settled more comfortably into his chair
and drew on his pipe with a show
of controlled satisfaction.
Behind him Edith looked like she would laugh,
but she turned her back on us all
and faced the window.

"Would you care for a brandy?" asked Travis,
and I said that I would,
and he poured me a measure from a cut-glass decanter
on the walnut sideboard.

"It's good stuff," said Travis as he carried it to me.
"I brought it back last Thursday from Avignon."
Their cat lay stretching itself on the window seat.
"Yes, there's good stuff in Avignon," said Travis,
and "You can say that indeed," said Denis,
and I think that he (Travis) winked
as he handed me the brandy.

"Here's to your good healths," I said to them all,
raising my glass in a sweeping gesture,
but "There must be," said Edith in a fierce whisper;
"you go there often enough."
"And to your new venture, Denis," I plodded on;
"may it thrive and prosper."

"Oh, there's no doubt about that," said Denis;
"I kept my wits about me these past six months,
and now everything's fallen into place."

"Just what do you mean by that, old girl?" said Travis,
replacing the cut-glass decanter on the sideboard
and moving behind Denis to confront Edith.
"Yes, you did do that," I replied to Denis
as "Oh nothing, of course," Edith answered,
and she bent down over the window seat,
and she picked up the cat.
"You must have meant something," he (Travis) responded;
"you always mean something whenever
you raise your eyebrow like that."

"Yes, I did do that," said Denis, "you can say that indeed,
and that's what I pride myself I've taught Travis to do,
as I think that these little trips of his
will be ample proof of."
Denis looked at the sideboard where Travis had been,
and he lifted his pipe as if to present a toast
or rather as if the motion conferred a blessing.
"Oh, go to hell," said Edith, and she threw the cat,
twisting and scratching, on Travis.

"Yes indeed," said Denis, leaning back in his chair
and smiling benignly, as it were, up at the ceiling
as Edith ran out of the room and Travis
said "Damn!" as he dropped the cat,
"there's no doubt as to what one can accomplish
when one keeps one's wits about one."

When I took Edie's place on the floor,
I saw that Les had somehow managed
to get back up on his feet.
He was moving his hands to a solemn music
only he could hear.
While Matthew nibbled on my ear and as Edie
crawled further under the table,
I scarcely noticed that Adrian—Allie's latest—
had come in with glasses and a bottle of scotch.

"This man looks like he needs a drink," said Adrian,
as he carefully stepped past Matthew and me
and handed a glass to Les.

Houses and Moons, Horses and Dogs

"He had a good third house," the speaker said,
"and a very strong fourth house," he added.
He pointed his long finger at us
as if we were the house.

I looked around me to see who else
wanted out of *this* house,
but seeing faces of rapt attention,
I studied the wallpaper instead,
where teams of horses pulled carriages
through tree-lined lanes.

"Now we all know that the fifth house,"
the speaker was saying as I tuned back in,
"is the house of hanky-panky."
He cocked his head sideways and smiled,
pausing a moment for our expected laughter.

"That sounds like a good house to me,"
I whispered to Joyce.
She, like the others, was laughing.

"Sshhh," she replied and patted my arm.
In each of the carriages meanwhile
sat the same well dressed couple.

"In the Indian system," the speaker went on
(after how many long long minutes
I could not tell you),
"the moon is activated in everyone's chart
by the age of twenty."

Well, it's too late for me, I thought.
For better or for worse mine
has been well activated.
And the chair I sat on was bony.

"I don't think she was the moon,"
the speaker was saying.
"His wife, I think, was the moon."
The others, including Joyce, received
this announcement with deep respect.

I leaned over and nudged Joyce with my shoulder.
"Will you be my moon?" I asked her,
and I made my tongue just visible between my lips
and took up her hand in mine.

"Not on your life," she hissed,
and she yanked it away.

Small dogs, beagles I think, were running
back and forth in front of the horses.
"He was ruler of the ninth house,
the luckiest of all houses," said the speaker.

"Well, not in this life anyway," Joyce relented,
smiling and giving me back her hand,
then making her tongue just visible
between her lips.

A Hole in the Clouds

I dragged myself to the edge of the roof
and spit into a warm breeze
which carried it back to the house.
It landed on my sister's bedroom window, I think,
and I had to laugh.

And laugh I did as I rolled over
and watched a hole in the clouds
where the sun slipped through.
The radio was right, there would
be a change in the weather.

And then I heard Mother calling my name again,
as she'd done just minutes before
and also just minutes before
minutes before.
This time she came outdoors
and stood on the garden path,
her hands on her hips, or so I imagined,
looking left and right.
Oh, climb up the hickory tree, Mother,
and you'll see your son.
You can see your subject sprawled out
and scratching his back on the tiles.
You can sit on a branch and scold his lazy hide
till your tongue turns black in your mouth.

Well, she didn't climb up the tree,
and I had to laugh
as I heard her go into the kitchen.

I laughed and I laughed as the sun
warmed me all over.
Then I rolled to my side and saw that the geese
had finished splashing themselves in the high water.
They were marching back up the hill, heads high,
in perfect formation, one following the other.

His Words

All afternoon he spoke of the gospel makers,
of their great power in carrying the words,
of the great debt of those who receive the words.
He never mentioned Our Lord
without praise for those who carried the words.

Then the small group dwindled,
thinning through boredom, hunger, or thirst,
till only a few of us stayed on
to listen by early starlight.
"The words," he said, "are the words
only when they are the words of great power.
No other words will do."

And then by a moon obscured,
when I alone stayed on to listen,
the scoffers having all departed,
he scattered the sparks of his wood fire
and marched with me to my tent.

We marched past the nuptial camp
of the honeymoon couple,
lost in their mindless sleep;
and we marched past the ignorant men
on their college break
who passed the days with cards
and with cases of beer.
"None of them are yet ready," he said,
and dismissed them all with a circling sweep of his
    arm.

* * *

That night, he lodged his spirit
in my receptive flesh.
In the morning, he cut my hair,
and he trimmed my beard.
In the morning, he washed my body
with water he carried from the river.
In the morning, he tore up my books
and destroyed my tapes.

"The words must be right," he said,
"and the words must be new,
and you will carry them for me,
mouth to mouth."

At noon, he rode forth,
wearing one of my shirts and a pair of my jeans,
having burnt his own.
For the past two days I have fasted,
and morning and evening,
I have bathed in water from the river.

The ranger has noticed my missing bike,
but that's no concern of his.
My time is up at the end of the week.
Then he will come riding back—
at the end of the week—
and together we'll sweeten this world
with his good news.

Hard-Won Gifts

Sometimes Father will just be standing there,
shoulders collapsed,
hands busy wiping themselves
on his vest,
eyes behind thick lenses
flat and ungrasping.

And sometimes Rose stands beside him.
She helps him into a chair
at the small table,
then places a hand on his arm.
Together, they are stationed to face down
the intrusion.

Mother is never there.
Or Jimmy, or Mark, or Uncle Peter.
Their existence itself is tentative,
their location unsure.

I don't know why I always
feel it this way,
why hard-won gifts weigh heavy
in my hopeless hands,
why select phrases, like fishbones,
stick in my throat.

A Good Snort

"Actually I'm looking
at your tamed eyebrows,"
she said.

"You look almost as cute now
as you did fifty years ago this day,"
she went on.

"Hrrff," I snorted.
At moments like these the only response
is a good snort.

"Here let me straighten your tie," she said.
She moved in closer and she jerked my tie
this way and that.

Then—wouldn't you know it?—
she found some speck on my collar
to brush off with her fingers.

"You don't mind if I fuss a bit?" she asked.
She picked up the scissors again,
and this time she went for my moustache.

She smelled as good as new, I must say,
with her powders and oils and whatever else,
and she had on a dress I didn't remember seeing.

"Keep your hands to yourself," she commanded,
proving once more her unfair ability
to read my mind.

Just then the doorbell rang.
"Oh God," she said, "the kids are here already.
Do I look all right? You haven't said how I look."

"You look just fine," I told her,
"but you'll look better when all this bother is over
and I see you naked."

"Lord, what a man," she said.
"How little I knew, fifty years ago,
what I was getting into."

"Hrrff," I snorted.

54

The Gift

"What's that in your hand?"

"Which hand are you talking about?" I asked her.

"Which hand indeed!" she replied, her voice rising
and her hair tossing as she stamped her foot.
"I don't suppose it could be the hand
you're holding behind your back."

"Oh that one," I said, twisting to keep her from seeing.
"Give me a hug and I'll show it to you.
Give me a kiss and it's yours."

"No thanks," she said, yawning
and sitting back down at her easel.
"I imagine it's nothing I'd care for."
She picked up a brush and jabbed at the tree
in the middle of her canvas.

"You'll ruin that tree," I said
and stepped close enough to place my chin on her shoulder.
"Would you like to guess what it is?"

"Oh that's easy enough," she said
as she shrugged and pushed me away.
"I imagine you're holding a black and white photo
of an epileptic Hari Krishna."

"Correct," I said and kissed the top of her head.
"He's tall and he's naked and he's standing on a Ford Escort."
I ran a forefinger down the side of her neck.

"You're awful," she said, grabbing hold of my finger.
"No one imagines a Ford Escort."
Then she daubed green paint on my hand.

"You're right as always," I sighed,
and I wiped my hand as best I could on the grass
before I gave her the daisy.

The Game

"Okay," said Jan, pushing back her chair,
"now listen to me."
I almost choked on my stew.
What else had we done all day?

We'd listened to Jan when we loaded Frank's car
and she told us what to put where.
We'd listened to Jan on the turnpike
as she told us the rules of the game we
would play that night.

And now here we were, still listening.
I had said to Frank all along
that it wasn't a good idea,
that I didn't much like the ad he had answered.
I'd told him, but here we were.

So I wiped some stew from my chin—it was canned stew—
and interrupting the launch of paragraph forty,
I stood up from the table.
Holly gave me a funny little smile, I thought,
as I walked out the door.

There was one good hour of daylight left.
The grass in the clearing was a wet green,
and the evergreens sparkled in the late afternoon sun.
Jan had said there were trout in the stream
and we might see deer.

Back in the cabin, I found Jan sweeping the floor,
wearing an apron that was longer than her skirt.
"Help yourself to a beer," she said.
"Holly and Frank are bringing in the wood.
Your job, if you're not too busy, is to build a fire.
And I'll be making the beds."

The beds, I didn't like thinking of the beds.
I had to admit that Jan was prettier than Holly—
she had smoother skin, she had straighter teeth,
and she had a more noteworthy ass—
but the last thing I wanted to do that night
was to share her bed.

So I went to the fridge for a beer.
"I'll just have to win Jan's game," I said to myself,
twisting the cap from the bottle.
"If it's the last thing that ever I do,
even if I have to cheat,
I'm winning the game."

Funny Stories

I try to get her new boss to loosen up,
telling him funny stories about Nettie,
like the time a barb wire fence
pulls her out of her skirt
or the time she falls on her ass
while feeding the pigs.
(I make that one up.)

All he can manage is a skinny smile
or at best a heh heh.
Not the sound of heh heh, mind you,
but the words heh heh,
as if he was reading from the funnies.

He's wearing a light blue sports coat from Sears,
and the dirt path to our house hasn't knocked
the shine from his new brown shoes.
He sits where I put him in Dad's old rocker
without touching its arms,
and he places his hands on his knees.
He's the high stepper, no doubt,
of the local lodge.

Then Nettie comes in at last
with her hair all curled
and wearing a made-over party dress of Mother's.
She sweeps into the room like a teen-age prom queen
rehearsing her big entrance to the big dance.

"Don't you have jobs to do?" she asks me,
as her caller rises stiffly to take her hand,
and she makes me a face as they waltz to the door.
Then I watch from the window as he puts her into his car,
she smiling as if she's won some prize
and ready, I see, to go and get herself
de-virginised again.

The Fountain in the Market Place

Andrew stood by the fountain
in the market place,
and Christine took his picture.
The fountain was small
with some floral decoration
at the lip of the basin
and bits of rubbish collected
along the rim.
The market was large but quiet,
its stands closed up for the night.
A few rib-thin dogs
were sniffing for scraps.
Dust moved about our feet
in erratic spirals.

Christine had a Polaroid camera,
and she handed over to me
its view of Andrew.
He stood tall by the fountain
with hands in his pockets,
a sizeable smile on his face.
If Christine had taken my picture,
I too would have stood tall
beside the fountain;
I too would have smiled.
But she didn't suggest it,
and I bought them some wine
in a small wineshop we found
in a nearby square.

A Fork in the Road

At a fork in the road Judith paused,
and I stopped behind her.
She looked a long time to the right
where the road passed into the dusty shrubs
and narrowed from vision.
Then she looked a long time to the left
where the road curved into the hillside
and disappeared.
I shifted my burden from one
shoulder to the other
and looked down at my feet.

When I raised my eyes again, Judith had not moved
except that now she was looking
down at her feet.
Perhaps she was studying the small red flowers
rooted in the middle of the road.
Perhaps, like me, she was simply
looking down at her feet.

I'm sitting here now, leaning against my pack
and writing my name in the dust with a twig.
For God's sake, Judith, do something.
Small lizards dart through the coarse grass,
and a breeze is rising as the sun
sinks into the shrubs.
Judith is no longer looking down at her feet.
Instead she looks off to the right, as if for an answer.
Then she looks off to the left.

Forecasts

"Are you nearly ready?"
Ready for what? I said to myself,
looking at the shoe in my hand and not at Blanche.
"Well, are you?" she asked again,
one hand on the doorknob and her green umbrella
gripped in the other.

"As ready as I'll ever be," I told her
and was sorry as soon as I saw the look
that passed over her face.
(A very pretty face, I have to admit,
except when she blanched—if you'll pardon a bad joke.)
I put on the shoe and stood to attention, smiling.

In the street, children were playing ball
with such urgency one could suppose
that the chance might never recur.
Ahead of us somewhere, an alarm sounded,
and grimy scraps were blowing along the pavement,
collecting wherever they caught.

That was my last afternoon with Blanche.
We arrived at the park in time, despite her predictions,
but the show had to be cancelled when the heavy rain
complied with the forecast.
We huddled together at a small concession stand
where I paid for hot dogs and weak coffee
with the last of my cash.
Later we took the path around the pond,
where we saw a rain-soaked couple
holding hands and laughing at the ducks.

There are moods that pass in a minute, I suppose,
and others that shape our futures.
Nor Blanche nor I spoke a word on the walk back,
not even when a passing van
splattered my legs.
The children had all disappeared,
leaving for us the sodden scraps on the pavement.
They were spots of uncertain white
in the gathering gloom.

A Fierce Wind

The wind blew fierce against the house,
nearly a gale.
I stood by the stove.
The cold had entered my bones
as I strode through the sodden field
to check on the goats
and then, returning, as I faced
into the rain.

I placed my kerosene lamp on the table—
the power was still off—
and I hung my coat by the stove.
Thick as it was, my coat
hadn't been enough,
but at least it had kept away
the drops of water now pooling
on the concrete floor.

I opened the door of the stove
where wood sizzled and spat
in the fire we had kept burning
for the past nine days.
I warmed my hands.

But where was Annie?
I listened and I couldn't hear her.
"Hey, Annie," I called, "I'm back";
but all I could hear in reply
was the wind, the crackling wood,
and the draught up the flue.

Then I saw our big pot on the stove
and, lifting the lid,
I found both the rabbits I had snared
swimming in a boil of carrots and spuds.
We would have enough stew for ourselves
and for all the dogs on the mountain.

Then I looked in the bedroom and Annie wasn't there,
and I looked out the window at the kennels
and I saw no lamp,
and I looked in the room we'd shut up
at the end of summer.

There, the table was laid
with places for six,
and candles placed on the sideboard
threw shadows on the cold and damp
recesses of the room.

Much later, after the dogs
came on Annie's body,
I found the note she had left me:
"Back soon. Gone for flowers."
It lay on the floor, another scrap of paper
blown to the wall where we stacked our firewood.

The Fields of Corn

She says nothing, and she looks away.
By away, I mean she looks out the window.

By out the window, I mean she looks out
over the expanse of well-kept grass,
past the ceramic fawns at the edge of the drive,
and into the fields of corn.

Assuming, of course, that her eyes are open.

What I see of her is her back, her shoulders squared,
her smock falling loose on her heavy body,
its patterns bright to her knees.
She's cheerful enough in the colours she wears.

What I imagine I see is the pursed mouth,
the affronted pride in her steamy eyes.
I saw them often enough whenever our mother
attempted to budge her.

"Well, have it your way," I say—I don't know why.
I suppose that in spite of it all
I feel sorry for the slut.

Still she says nothing, and still she looks away.
By away, I mean she looks out past the fields of corn
and into the time when she'll have it
all to herself.

Assuming, of course, that she lives that long.

A Few Words

"I don't just bandy my lines around," she said.
"I don't just serve them up for the likes of you
or any other hero who comes mooching along
with the tongue of his biro hanging out."

She was joking, of course, I could see that,
though there was an edge to her voice
and something of a challenge in her dark eyes.
The men behind me at the bar were suddenly quiet,
and I wondered were they listening in.
What had happened to the talk of Sunday's match?
And where had the weather gone to?

"It's just a few words," I said, "that's all,"
but she drained off her gin and tonic
without taking her eyes from mine.
"My words," she said, putting down her glass,
"and you have them on that piece of paper."

"No longer," I said, crumpling up the paper
and throwing it into the fire, on the burning coals.
"I consign your words to oblivion," I added.

She stared at the fire as the paper turned brown,
and she started to reach her hand toward the grate.
Then the paper burst into flames.
"Those words of yours are hot stuff," I said.

When I spoke, she snapped shut the pain on her face.
"My round," she said, digging into her purse.
"Are you having the same?"

An Evening to Ourselves

I felt relieved that no one
was in the house.
We'd have the evening to ourselves.
I could see us eating a quiet supper in the garden
where I could tell Beryl about my plan
for reduction of inventory,
and Beryl could describe her new sketches
for the fall displays.
Then after a brandy or two,
we could enter the sweet dream of an early night
with limbs aligned and hearts beating as one.

This music repeated itself as I showered
and changed into jeans and a T-shirt.
My mood was on hold as I made my way to the kitchen
where it was now time to toss a salad
and put on water for pasta.
Any minute now I would hear Beryl's car pool
dropping her off at the end of the drive.

What I didn't expect to find
was the large tea pot,
down from the cupboard, squatting beside the stove,
and sadly, treacherously warm.
In failing health, I pushed open the back door,
and there were Portia and Bruce, friends from the city,
and their two precocious daughters, Jodi and Pearl.
It was going to be a diverting weekend.

"Yoo hoo, Freddy, yoo hoo," Portia was calling
while bravely waving her cup,
"Beryl's driving our Audi to the village for wine,
and we're out here in the garden."

Eva Braun and My Sister Val

I nodded at Val, pretending to consider her request,
but she saw through the ruse.
"Well, at least you could feed your cat," she said,
her face scarcely large enough for the hurt
which ran out to its edges.

Eva Braun, who had given up making a fuss,
no doubt agreed.
She glared at me from a wicker chair
where she lay in a heap, curled and sullen,
her bad thoughts outnumbering her fleas.

"Even if you don't give a damn about Mother and me,"
Val added lamely.
The quaver in her voice suggested she'd soon
be entering a weepy stage,
so I rose with a parody of effort,
knocking over my chair,
and went for the catfood.
Eva Braun, in an altered humour,
got there before me.

All that was some minutes ago, and now Eva Braun
stretches out on my lap, a picture of female contentment.
"Animal Relaxation," I think you could call it.
Soon enough she'll have to move on,
when I get up to shave,
but for just now I'm stroking my cat
while I listen to Val in the bathroom
still blubbering and washing her face.

Elsie

Elsie tossed her head in contempt
and then went out in the hallway to ring Kevin.
I could hear the coins drop in the slot
and then the dial turn on the old-style phone.
Then I heard, or imagined I heard,
the ringing she listened to during the long pause.
Finally I heard the coins return.
I knew, as Elsie could not have known,
there would be no answer,
but when she came back into her room,
I said nothing to her.
She could think whatever she decided to think.

But the Elsie that returned was a less confident Elsie.
I watched her close as she drifted across the room.
For a moment she stood undecided by the dresser,
and then she pulled her blouse up over her head
and laid it across a chair.
I watched as she stepped carefully out of her skirt
and placed it too on the chair.
She didn't look once in my direction
but stood turned away, facing the wall.
"Unhook me?" she said.

Afterwards, Elsie lay sleeping on the bed settee
while I lay stretched on the floor, examining the carpet.
It hadn't been worth my trouble, I said to myself,
for Elsie, to speak the truth, was a disappointment.
I might even say so to Kevin one day.
One day when I'm feeling hurtful.

I can move as quiet as any cat when I want to.
I rose from the floor and put on her blouse and skirt,
leaving my own clothing where I had dropped it.
It was hardly a fair exchange
but something for Elsie to remember me by.
She stirred only slightly as I crossed the room
and slipped out the door.

A Dirty Smudge

There was a high front from somewhere,
said the voice in the other room,
and I could imagine the pointer
tapping the map.
Another high front was from someplace else,
the voice informed me.
No doubt the pointer was being
equally useful.

I left the sink for the kitchen doorway,
and there in the other room was the map
with the nation divided by curving lines
and labelled with circles and arrows.
There too, as I had imagined,
was the man with the pointer.
His intent, circumspect smile
was aimed past my shoulder.

I wiped my sleeve over beads of sweat
collected above my eyebrows.
Those two highs would be merging, he announced
as I left the doorway.

Back in the kitchen I put my hands
deep in the hot, greasy water
till I found the casserole dish.
Then with a scouring pad I worked
on the egg or meat or cheese or whatever
that was stuck to the sides and bottom.
Sweat collected again on my brow,
and on the lino was a dirty smudge

where I'd stepped into spilled water.
Maybe I'd take a mop to the floor.
Maybe I wouldn't.

Whatever it means, I said out loud
as I let go the casserole dish,
those two highs will be merging tonight.
I'm in a space cut off by curving lines,
labelled with circles and arrows.

Dinner with Monica

Bob piled our plates on the tray
and carried them off to the kitchen.
It was then we heard the prolonged
and unmistakable sputter
of a pent-up fart.

It gave us an awkward minute
during which Monica studied her place mat;
and then she asked brightly if Bob
did much of the cooking.
"Oh yes," I replied, "Bob cooks on weekends
and sometimes on special occasions.
It's your luck that you happened by
on one of his nights."

"My luck indeed," said Monica.
"That artichoke salad was splendid."

Bob came in then with the main course,
Cornish Hens Mandarin with steamed bok choy.
We ate our fill as Monica enlarged
on her plans for the new boutique
she was opening in March.
The wine Bob had chosen was a brisk Chardonnay,
which seemed just the perfect companion
to Monica's excitement.

"We have only some leftover pear crisp for dessert,"
Bob said as he rose again to clear the dishes.
"Shall I bring it in with the coffee?"

Then he was off to the kitchen once more—
where we could hear him running the water tap
and scraping the plates into the garbage pail
and opening the pantry door
to fetch the pear crisp.

Monica's place mat, incidentally, offered
a view of the Grand Canal.
It was one of a set that my sister Claire
brought back from Venice.

A Dark Night

Noreen had invited the two of us for the weekend,
and now here we were
standing outside her cabin on a dark night
with wind blowing and snow promised on the radio.
I looked at Lambert and he looked at me.
Were we here on the wrong night?
Had she finished her novel already?
Had she simply forgotten?

We had passed through a town a few miles back.
Hardly a town really, just a few old stores
lined up along the road, looking sad.
There was one café, which was closed, and no tavern.
The gas station looked open,
but I hadn't seen any sign there of Noreen's bike.
I wasn't exactly looking for it, of course.

"We'll try the windows," said Lambert, and he did just that.
They were locked as tight as the door.
"God damn it anyway," he said,
"if that gas station has closed, we're in deep shit."
Then he kicked the door of the cabin so hard
I thought he would smash it.
"We haven't enough gas to get back to the city,
so what do you say we break a window?" he asked.

I looked at Lambert for what must have been
the five hundredth time.
I like a man with hair, and his full beard
was matched by black hairs all over his wrists.

In my thoughts they covered his chest and ran down his belly,
but I never expected to find out.
"Or maybe you'd rather spend a freezing night
huddled in my God damn car?" he demanded.

"If your body is half as hot as your God damn temper,
then maybe I wouldn't mind it," I answered,
but I said this only to myself.
And it's a good thing, too, for just then
Noreen came out of the woods, walking a dog.

"You might have left a light on for us," said Lambert,
by way of greeting,
as she all but vanished in his arms.

The Compliments

The compliments around here would knock you dead,
but what to make of them is the question.
Bennie especially keeps hanging around me,
painting my picture in words
like a dog with a wagging tongue
who's looking for a good sniff.

"Oh, like enough," I tell him, and "go on with you,"
letting him know I'm not some little fool
to be taken in by his talk.

And all the time I'm trying to look at the horses
and some of the lads that's on them,
I see he's checking out my boobs
and the cut of my new jeans.

Then Doreen comes nosing in,
telling me our da wants us home for tea,
so I have to leave Bennie to look at the horses by himself
—or maybe at some little fool
who'll listen to him say how good she's looking
all dickey-dooed.

The show jumping itself wasn't all that great,
if I'm honest with you,
but the compliments around there
would knock you dead.

The Company

"It's not the hour," she said, yawning. "It's the company."
And with that she rose from her chair.
We sat there absorbing what we both hoped
was another of her jokes.

As she stood, still yawning, she stretched,
and her green blouse rose taut
to reveal the shape of her breasts.
Her raven hair, disarrayed, fell back from her face,
and beneath her wide open mouth we could see
the lines of her long, pale neck.
Then she crossed the room with her glass,
which she placed on the table.

"Stay up as long as you like," she said.
"There's more beer in the fridge, if you want it,
and there's coffee on the stove.
I've laid out some towels in your bedroom."
As she crossed the floor to the stairway,
we muttered good night and our thanks for dinner.
"Oh, sleep as late as you like," she added.
"I'm not on duty till two."

With that she ascended the stairwell,
and we watched as her feet negotiated each slow step,
my husband, to be sure, as full of yearning as I was.
In the silence that followed the closing of a door upstairs,
we listened for footsteps, for a cough, for the dropping of a shoe.

Cleo

"Will you look at your fly," said Cleo,
and I looked down where Cleo was pointing
and saw it was open.
"Your yellow Jockeys are showing," she said,
giggling and covering her mouth
with her other hand.

From the other side of the door, meanwhile,
a woman's voice kept saying,
"Just a minute, Cleo, just a minute,
I've dropped the key."

"Oh dear," said Cleo, suddenly grim,
"if Mums sees you like this, she'll say that you're
another one I found on the dump."

"Well thanks a lot," I said
while I fought with the zipper,
which in my haste I had managed
to snag on my shorts.

"Instead," she continued, her voice tightening,
"of seeing you for what you are."

"Which is what?" I demanded as Cleo
took over pulling on my zipper.

"My one accomplishment," said Cleo,
tears threatening her cheeks
as the door swung open.

The Chinese Bowl

I didn't hear the front door at all,
either when she let herself in
or when she let herself out,
but I was in the kitchen cleaning the fridge.
Besides, as I had occasion to know,
Amy Burns could be as quiet as any mushroom.

When I did, later, walk into the living room,
it was only by chance that I came across
the gifts I had given her.
She had placed them all in the Chinese bowl
that I keep on the corner shelf.
Baffled, estranged, and disavowed,
I sat down on the floor and turned them over in my hands.

Some time later, toward noon,
I was still on the floor, the gifts spread out on my palms,
when the door opened with a whisper
and there stood Amy Burns.
For a long minute we just stared at one another.
She was wearing her light blue dress
and a dark blue brooch which set off her pale throat.
I think I saw beads of moisture springing up
at the corners of her eyes.
I think she looked disappointed as she backed away,
closing the door behind her.

Perhaps I should have called out to her then,
"Come back, it's all right,"
and followed her into the street.
Instead I walked back to the kitchen
and poured out a glass of milk with unsteady hands,
spilling some drops on the counter.

The last time I dusted the Chinese bowl,
the gifts were still there where I replaced them.
I consider that they belong to Amy Burns.
Moreover, they're not my style.

The Chevy

"At the end of your rope you'll find Jesus."

"What's that you said?" I asked,
swinging my Honda into the passing lane
and blasting my horn at the Chevy
straddling the white line.

She fetched a brush from her string bag
and attacked her hair for the third or fourth time
since we left the motel.
"At the end of your rope you'll find Jesus,"
she repeated slowly.
"I was reading another of those billboards."

She put back the hairbrush and yawned.

Two little girls in the back of the Chevy
waved as we shot by them,
and one of them stuck out her tongue.
Ahead of us stretched an endless empty highway
with nothing much to the sides
but rocks and sagebrush and sand.

"You cut in front pretty close, don't you think?"
She patted my knee to lessen the accusation,
and she placed her hand on my thigh.
"You got a grudge against Chevys?" she added.

We were reaching the crest of a long slow grade,
and the Chevy grew gradually smaller
in the rear-view mirror.

"What's he doing there at the end
of my rope?" I asked her.
"Is he hanging by the neck?"

"You've been driving too long," she said,
removing her hand and reaching again
for her string bag.

A Can of Beer

I sat there cooling my hands on a beer can.
"There's one here for you, too, if you want it," I said
and fetched one out of the water.

Her answer was an unintelligible grunt,
and I saw that she had one sock in her mouth
as she put on the other.
She was sitting on a large rock at the edge of the river,
and the bright sun at her back
made a red halo of her hair.

"Your hair is lovely," I said
and I drained my beer can,
"but if you're not drinking this other beer yourself,
I'll drink it for you."

She took the sock out of her mouth and laughed.
"Well, if that's the best you can do," she said,
"I will have that beer."

"No, I really mean it," I answered,
"your hair *is* lovely.
You should see how it looks just now
with the sun behind it."

"Well, I can't do that, can I?" she said,
putting on the sock,
then standing up on the rock and brushing off dust.
"Now hand me my beer if you please.
And if I were you, I'd put on my shirt.
You're beginning to look like a lobster."

Breakfast at the Hotel

"I work in this hotel actually,"
Tommy explained,
"though I wasn't on duty last night ... of course."
The last of his sentence was aimed at the napkin
wadded in his hand.

"So do I," said Glenda, plopping onto her plate
the last of the caramel rolls.
"That's what I was doing last night anyway."
She turned toward me, licking her fingers
and smiling as if for confirmation.
Then she began on her roll.

The sun was breaking out, so I rose from the table
and made my way through a scattering of shoes
to the balcony door.
When I pulled back the patterned drapes,
I found bright snow on the airy hills;
and far below I could see white splotches
that I took to be sheep.
Seen from this new perspective, the world
had plenty of sparkle.

"Is there more coffee?" asked Tommy,
breaking a long silence,
and I turned and watched Glenda filling his cup.
The two of them looked rather funny and sweet
in my flannel shirts.

"I'll be taking a shower now," I told them,
"but take your time over coffee, there's no hurry."
I felt their eyes on my back as I crossed the room.

"Of course, if either of you cares
to join me," I added,
"it's safe to say there'll be plenty
of hot water."

The Box

Ellie continued to look at the box
which her visitor had left.
It was, I assumed, a token of regard,
perhaps of affection,
but Ellie had barely smiled
when he handed it to her.
I thought she looked vexed as he bent his grey head
to kiss her cheek.

It had the proportions of a shoe box
but was somewhat smaller.
It was papered in gaily coloured tissue
with bright, primal flowers
suitable for the time of year, May Day.
(Unlike the weather—a cold, driving rain.)

As Ellie continued just looking, I busied myself,
adding wood to the fire and then fetching
my boots and my slicker.
To delay departure, I opened my purse
and looked for my keys.
Then I went to the bathroom and blew my nose.

When I returned to the kitchen, Ellie hadn't moved.
The overhead bulb flickered off, then on, and then off.
Our terrier, curled on its bedding, stirred
and moaned in a dream.
Ellie reached for the paring knife
and severed the string.

Ellie would never explain what she did next.
She crossed the room and dropped the string on the fire,
and then she added the box.
I watched the pansies and the buttercups,
or whatever they were,
peel away in flame;
and then the fire began on the box
as a corner of the cardboard blackened and then flared,
casting light and shadow.

The Boat

When I opened the curtains, it was my face
that I saw reflected in the window.
Not the face of my father
and not the face of my uncle Roy,
it was almost nobody's face,
being only my own.

Past this face, if I forced the view,
I could see the small boat tied to the dock
and beyond it the choppy water of a lake
where clouds gathered and darkened.
Why had I put off everything till this morning?

The clock in the entry started to clear its throat,
preparing to chime the hour,
and I knew without looking that the time was already seven.
I crossed to the stove for another cup of black coffee,
to which I added all that was left of the whiskey.

The boat was a sweet little boat,
it was damned near perfect,
and I knew Uncle Roy had chosen it well.
But back at the window, I saw only a fragile craft
tethered to the dock of a large, threatening lake.
In front of it all was the face of a man
with his nerves up against the wall,
the face of a man turned inside out.

The Blue Blouse

Susan threw the sweater across the room,
but then stood riveted listening to the phone.
When I started to pick it up, she screamed,
so I let it ring.
Just as well, I thought, just as well.
It was probably Bobbi.

Susan was wearing one of my blouses,
a pale blue cotton which matched her eyes,
but then she'd worn it so often
she may have convinced herself
it was hers by right.
The last time that I had it on,
she gave me a look as if to say
it was done by permission.

I hate a scene like the one we were having,
especially if it bothers my work.
It gives me a bad stomach and I don't perform well.
"Damn you, Susan," I told her again,
"will you just listen?
Bobbi was worried about her opening line
in the last act,
so we went to the bar after the show
and we talked about it."

You'd think that Susan, after all this time,
would at least listen,
but it's seldom she does—or did.
Instead, she covers her ears with her hands,
and when I open my mouth to speak,
she screams again.

She was screaming as I smacked her across the face,
and even louder as I wrestled her
out of the blouse.
"That sweater is yours if you want it," I said.
"Take it with you when you clear out."

I walked through the door with the torn blouse in my hand
and a cramp in my gut.
"And happy birthday," I shouted back at her
from the top of the stairwell.

Ben

Ben found that he could no longer
speak to Donald.
That's what he told me later.
Later when he brought himself
to tell me about it.

He blamed Donald more than himself
and more than the disappointing game,
the drinks at the club, the bitter cold night,
the nearness of Donald's rooms.

Donald the Seducer.

It was a warm night in mid May
by the time Ben told me.
He hemmed and hawed all through dinner
till I feared that at long last
I must hear about it.

Worst of all, Ben
would plead
for forgiveness.
And then I would have to forgive him
and show that I meant it.

To put off that privileged moment
I kept rising from the table.
To open the kitchen door and let in the cat.
To put the broiler pan to soak in the sink.
To check out a strange noise
in the children's bedroom.

But Ben kept looking more solemn.
And picked at his food.
And suggested we sit in the garden.
Where he cleared his throat,
took hold of my hand,
and looked me straight in the eyes.

It was more fun, I can tell you,
when I heard it from Donald.
Donald gave me a dozen laughs
as we warmed ourselves by his fire.
While cold air blew in through his rattling windows
and snow beat hard on the panes,
how descriptive he was—
recalling Ben's awkward passion
and then his remorse.

Well that's my Ben, of course.
And that's why I love him.

Being Careful

I put my hand carefully on the doorknob,
and I carefully turned it.
That doorknob was connected
to the door of our guest room.
There was still time to change my mind,
but I guess I didn't.

I was only trying to be careful,
just as I had been careful at dinner
not to look at Uncle Lester.
Or at least not to let Mother see how much
I was looking at him.
Mother says that not seeming to look
is something I've gotten good at.

I have a white dress I almost never put on.
Mother won't let me wear it without a slip,
and I hate wearing slips.
It wouldn't fit me today, but that night
it slid all over my skin
as I slipped through the door.
The floor felt cold to my bare feet
till I came to the throw rug.

Uncle Lester was sleeping
in a pair of blue pyjamas
that had been my father's.
He wasn't, if it makes any difference,
really my uncle.

Mother says you can never be too careful.
Well, I was careful that night
to place my hand gently on Uncle Lester's mouth
when I woke him up.

A Bed in the Parlour

I stepped forwards and clutched at the railing,
but I was too late.
As the loose gravel gave way, I looked at James,
our eyes locking as he reached for my arm.
Too late.

On my way down, I tumbled
through chubby white sheep with black faces
and a cluster of furze.
My eyes had locked with James's eyes
as he reached to detain me.
The furze broke my fall.
How hard, I asked, had James tried?

Now they've made me a bed in the parlour,
and I lie here all day, surrounded by stuffy brocade,
overseen by the portrait of James's great-aunt Maggie.
From time to time a dutiful James appears,
genial and nervous,
with one of my friends in tow.
Later I hear them laughing with his mother
over tea in the kitchen.

The sheep were large and dirty and they shied away.
The furze were spiny and tore at my arms,
but they broke my fall.
From time to time I ask my question out loud,
but Great-Aunt Maggie, her mouth as mute as my heart,
has nothing to say.

Auspicious

We're young and happy and auspicious,
and that's where we'll stay,
but you wouldn't have seen it last night.
"Do you still love me?" she asks,
just as she's pulling back the covers
and I'm opening a condom.

"Of course I love you," I say,
lying down and stretching on my back.
"Come here and I'll show you."

She hangs her robe on a hook and just stands there,
naked under the bare bulb
with the shadows under her breasts
spreading down the curve on her stomach
and pointing to her mound of hair.
"But am I still attractive?" she asks,
her eyes aging as she lowers her head
and surveys her body.

"Of course you're attractive," I say. "Why do you ask?"
I rise up sideways on my elbow,
and I stick out my tongue and ogle.

She doesn't even crack a smile.
"How much do you love me?" she asks, her voice
        growing dim.
She still hasn't gotten into bed.

"Oh, how do I know?" I say.
"I love you as much as the moon," I say.
"Now, are there any more questions?" I say.
She bursts into tears.

"This condom costs 50¢, that's how much I love you."
I spit this out of my mouth
as she lifts her robe off the hook
and puts it back on.

All the Makings

I was going to tell her,
but she looked so fresh and happy in her red dress
that I hadn't the heart.
Perhaps I could do so later.

But why was she wearing her new dress
for a dinner at home?
I hung my coat in the closet with this question in mind,
and I carried it with me into the john,
where I sweetened the porcelain.
After nearly five years of marriage, Jess
was still full of surprises.

Then "Happy Anniversary, Darling," she said
as I took my seat at the table;
and then Shit!—I said to myself—
it's been five full years.
My stomach, as they say, turned over
at the full horror.

"You forgot, my darling," she said,
misreading my stunned reaction,
"but it doesn't matter."
She reached for my hand, and I had to squeeze
hers in return.

On her wrist was the turquoise bracelet
I'd given her the year before.
To the left of her plate was a small box
half hidden behind the pepper,
meticulously tissued.

There were red candles on the table,
and the light of love, as they say, shone bright
in her sea-green eyes.

It had all the makings of a prolonged
and romantic evening.
The meal no doubt would be good
and the wine perfect.